CRIMSON VAPOR

Nicholas Fisher

Crimson Vapor copyright © 2019 by NIcholas Fisher
All rights reserved.

cvmarshen@gmail.com

Boulder, Co.

ISBN-13: 978-0-578-46493-0

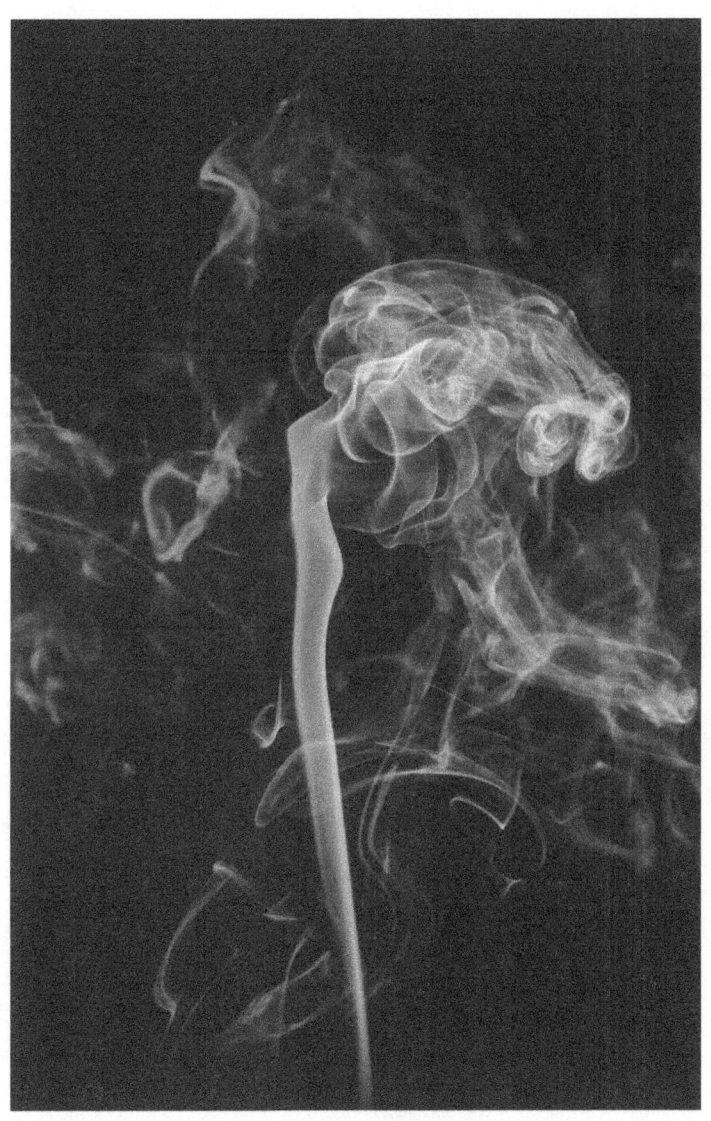

Crimson Vapor

TABLE OF CONTENTS

PURPLE ------------------------------- P.10

TURQUOISE ---------------------------- P.41

GREEN -------------------------------- P.53

ORANGE ------------------------------- P.69

LIGHT BLUE --------------------------- P.83

DARK BLUE ---------------------------- P.97

RED ---------------------------------- P.117

MAROON ------------------------------- P.139

"I aint know if there were normal rules to this shit.
 I just want to explain where these writings came from, that I was writing through a depression.
I realized I aint love myself and found myself through being lost.
Also, I have to point out the fact that I feel my pens had energies & I was getting attached to them, so I needed to give them 'names'"
-/ˈmärSHən/

"Respect!!! Make sure you add that in there too!!
Just like that!
Be yourself throughout this whole process.
You're going to change people's lives."- ProVerb

PURPLE

<u>PAIN</u>
This is my most famous pen
The one that knows me best
The reason I needed more colors in my life
To fill this void in my chest
I'm trying to detach from it
But it's still a part of my life
One of my best teachers yet
Pain
-/ˈmärSHən/

Late night fires that burn down to an ember
The main cause for my sleepless November
Slow monotonous breaths until my lungs can filter the smoke
Another day passes and the ember ignites,
Causing me to choke
I'm walking around with covert napalm burns
Because forgiveness is the hardest lesson to learn.
-/ˈmärSHən/

You're a distant memory
No longer tangible, just only in my dreams to see
Half of the reason why I come home and rush to sleep
Hoping when I wake up, you'll be lying next to me
-/ˈmärSHən/

I've been stuck in this place for months,
Seems like I'm waiting for Godot
Begging for things to work out this once,
But those thoughts are inaudible
My eyes are heavy with depression and my sleep consist of nightmares
Waking to my death is a twisted therapy session
I'm stuck in my mind and there's no peace there
My brain is on its third week with no sleep...
-/ˈmärSHən/

TRUST ISSUES
The paranoia is what kills me
Not knowing if people have done
Those things in my head or not.
-/ˈmärSHən/

STRAWBERRY SUNDAYS
I'm missing you,

The way you had me smiling was ludicrous
You were the edifice of my inspiration
The reason I went to bed early
To wake up even earlier.
You were my source of happiness
You made my face glow and my ears tingle.

Had me dreaming about polychromatic sunflowers
Now you're just a soulful song I resonate with,
A song whose bass shakes my spirit

Red and blue creates purple

I write with pain.
-/ˈmärSHən/

HEALTHY AMOUNT OF SLEEP?
I see my thoughts on the ceiling
When my eyes are tired
And my mind is awake
-/ˈmärSHən/

B7
When I first saw you
it was like walking past a vending machine
seeing candy halfway over the coil,
I had to have you.
I was doing everything to get you to fall
And once I got you
I enjoyed you too much
Now you're just a memory
I know you were good, but I can't quite remember the taste
-/ˈmärSHən/

SENSITIVE
I have a way with words
And they have their way with me
When they are put together just right
They really get under my skin.
-/ˈmärSHən/

I forgot whose fault it was
For the way I am
Yours or mine?
All I know is scars like these take time
-/ˈmärSHən/

SLEEP PARALYSIS

I'll catch you in my nightmares
In the world with no light there
The devil you'll meet
And my demons, you'll meet too
These are my long nights
When the room is chilled and things
Are touching me but there's no one in sight
Talking in my sleep to the people on the other side
They all want you,
Until then I'll have to abide
Uninvited guest
-/ˈmärSHən/

SEASONAL
You love like the trees
Most of the time you're consistent
But when your love is most vibrant
You go bare, cold
Until things start getting warm again
-/ˈmärSHən/

CHARCOAL
Holding onto bad things and expecting
Something good is like touching fire and
Expecting not to get burned.
It's a risk, and we all take it
I guess I haven't learned my lesson
Because I'm burning.
-/ˈmärSHən/

I don't know how I can fall for it every time
I guess I just want to give things the benefit of the doubt
I deal with pain a lot better now than I used to
Sometimes I even find myself going against my own rules
Some people make you think it's worth it
No one is perfect and I understand that
I guess I'm getting to know grace, understanding, & forgiveness
Boy does the pain stick
I feel like I'm bound to live with a faulted heart
Or even one that doesn't get to thaw out
It's like lightning but in the worse way
I get struck and it volts through my body
Even though you forget what it feels like exactly
You know it still hurts like hell
It leaves you in the dirt every time
& over the days you become petrified
Little by little
Even with all of me fading
I still have pieces I try to give away
-/ˈmärSHən/

The seasons have changed
My body is going from cold to warm
But I'm begging for the winter to stay a little longer
-/ˈmärSHən/

REMNANTS
It's hard to think
We ever existed in the same breath
Our names were synonymous
If I was talking about you
I was talking about me
Harmonies to each other's melody
And now we sing separately
-/ˈmärSHən/

G.I. JOE

I remember it was dark
The air was frigid
And the sky was relieved of all its freckles
The night you told me you had to leave
You told me to be strong
And I cried
I didn't know what strength was then
The pain was incomprehensible
My tears were acid
And my eyes burned the entire night
-/ˈmärSHən/

The causes of my insomnia
Are the thoughts of my pain
-/ˈmärSHən/

STILL WON'T ASK FOR HELP
For my days of happiness
I have equal days of pain
The kind that makes your heart feel dry
And makes you want to walk outside
Wet
In the rain
Not even sleep can save me
I've been up at night
And my thoughts leave no hope in sight
My body is aching, and it comes from inside
And I don't say anything because I have a lot of pride
If I knew what was on the other side
I think I would have committed suicide
But the fact that its unknown
Is the reason I still come home

If you've been there before
Let me know.
-/ˈmärSHən/

Purple reign
Purple reign
It feels like chains
Captivating pain

That's what it feels like
To be insane
-/ˈmärSHən/

If my heart could talk
These pages would bleed
-/ˈmärSHən/

I'm not incapable of love or loving
But love hurts too much
To leave my heart in the hands
Of someone so reckless and thoughtless
-/ˈmärSHən/

You make it hard to believe that love exists
I question your good nature
I can't do anything without you twisting my wrist
But even that won't get me to feel for a stranger
-/ˈmärSHən/

I wish you could share these laughs with me
But you're in the skies
-/ˈmärSHən/

I'd rather you tell me you want to manipulate me
Instead of telling me you love me...
-/ˈmärSHən/

How could you say you love me?
Then commit such crimes against me
You smiled in my face
And still
You murdered my heart
-/ˈmärSHən/

Happiness is never what it seems
Smiles are deceptive
& mine aren't always what they are meant to be
-/ˈmärSHən/

A sense of belonging is what you're after
Without it you'd be shook to the core
Behind facades of laughter
Hiding pain from your internal war
-/ˈmärSHən/

My spirit reflected the house I grew up in
My sister was always out
Moms always at work
Pops protecting the country
Just like that house
I felt empty

Just my soul & me
& everyone else became the enemy
The bond of love was divorced before my first year on earth
You talking to a kid that thought love
Was synonymous with hurt

Like Luther said
A house is not a home
-/ˈmärSHən/

TURQUOISE

HEALING

This pen is for my deep breaths
My it's gonna be okays
For the nights I don't think the sun is gonna make it up
For the days I need someone in my corner
This pen will put the scabs on the wounds
That everyone has caused me
Including myself
-/ˈmärSHən/

COCOON
I was in darkness for a while
Fear took over
And I was bound on an elusive wonder
I thought I would be stuck in my form
Chained in a cell with myself
Talking to anger, rejection, and misunderstanding
As we passed around grudges
I did my time for resisting
An earthquake shook the foundation
My cell broke
My chains got lighter
And I flew
How do I live as a butterfly?
-/ˈmärSHən/

I used to feel alone all the time
Now I understand
I was meant to be alone
You helped me understand that
Through the talks we had
The conversations that mapped out feelings
I've been writing for many years
Not once did I look at it as healing
And now many days later
I think I'm ready to grow and expand
-/ˈmärSHən/

I see you
I see you beyond what you show to the world
I see you
I see you and that well of collective tears
I see you
I see through your almond eyes that hold all your emotion
I see you
I see your heart and all the mud it's been dragged through
I see you
I see you even though you have walls up
I pray you stay beautiful
Until all the world can see you
-/ˈmärSHən/

HANG IN THERE
I know most days are full of bliss
Then in one moment
Your brain reverts
& you start to reminisce
-/ˈmärSHən/

TATTOO JUNKIE
I needed some permanence in my life
So, I put ink into my body
The one thing that would never leave me
Upon what seemed to be destruction
-/ˈmärSHən/

I'm attracted to all things genuine
Because it's so hard to acquire it
-/ˈmärSHən/

I remember someone telling me
"I wanna love you'
& I remember thinking
"Wow, that's something I don't even know how to do"
-/ˈmärSHən/

I've found some things out
During my time away
That I would like to talk about
& the most important thing I have to say

I still haven't found myself
But I came to the realization
That I was lost
-/ˈmärSHən/

GREEN

GROWTH
This pen is to show I'm not in the same place I was yesterday
To show that I've gained perspective on my surroundings
This pen is the answer to everything that's been trying to keep me motionless
The pen to my growth
-/ˈmärSHən/

I'm drenched
I was moving down a quiet stream and my back was turned
I was no longer looking at the path I traveled
But up at the sky
Rapids shouting for my entrance
100 feet passed
200 feet passed
300 feet passed
I couldn't scream anymore
I lost my breath
A couple more hundred passed
And the chants got louder
The sky got further
And my fear got larger
Boom
I plunged in under the surface

And I raced to the top for air
But something held me there
It told me to listen
But I couldn't hear
It told me to rise
But I kept sinking
I started worrying about the life I had
Its grip loosened when I understood
Air wasn't the only thing my body needed
I was able to hear
When I started listening to peace
I started to rise
When I found happiness at the bottom
I emerged
I could breath
The waterfall almost conquered me
-/ˈmärSHən/

Because you are hurt
You must do the most growing
Not healing
You must understand not everyone is the same
Not everyone is out to give you that sick feeling
And not everyone's heart is full of pain
Because you are hurt
You must find the sunshine in the rain
On the days you forget your umbrella
You look to the sky instead
And listen to God's symphony
As those translucent drops descend from heaven
And fall on your head
-/ˈmärSHən/

For the plant whose stem is cut
I understand
You wanted a chance to grow like everyone else
But someone didn't see you fit for a blossom
And now you'll never have that opportunity
You lay on the ground
while some other flower uses your nutrients
So they can become pleasing to others
-/ˈmärSHən/

I don't want to be afraid to walk alone
Down paths with no imprints
Towards endings unknown
Where traces of success are not present
When this trail takes me to the cliff
Will I be brave enough to jump
Into the Smokey abyss
Or will it be my fluorescent speed bump
-/ˈmärSHən/

NO HARD FEELINGS
I can't get no reciprocation
If I'm giving all of me
You give me no appreciation
My heart is heavy
I need someone strong to hold it
I need someone with valleys of love to mold it
I can't get no reciprocation
If I'm giving all of me
You play me in your spare time
Like recreation
My mind is full of constellations
I need someone to make sense of it
Break down my walls
I don't want to play defense
The worst part is
If I'm giving all of me
It's with no expectations
You do me wrong
Because I'm not one of your obligations
-/ˈmärSHən/

Slash and burn
Cut down and set fire to my old ways
As the months pass and the skies rain
I will blossom again
-/ˈmärSHən/

You said you wouldn't
Lose yourself again
But here you are drowning
In a sea of anxiety

Gasping for a familiar reality
But you can't breathe in the new surroundings
And once more
You find yourself powerless
You're frantic
Don't panic
Or you'll sink
Quick
-/ˈmärSHən/

PHOENIX
Today I looked at my soul
& for once it smiled back at me
It's been a long time
Since I've been recognized through this hole
It's taken all this time for me to be set free
& through the ashes
 I stand on my feet
-/ˈmärSHən/

I'm comfortable with silence
Because I have conquered my demons
& withstood all their violence
With a smile on my face
Although my insides were screaming
-/ˈmärSHən/

What exactly is crimson vapor?
It's when your heart explodes
For the worse
& all that's left is mist
That paints stars with the darkest of reds
& causes planets to shift
It makes atmospheres uninhabitable
Through toxic waste
& the only way to make it better
Is to actively choose.
-/ˈmärSHən/

You have to put the right energy
In the right
Galaxies
Because some solar systems
Live off the black hole that feeds them
& if you aren't careful
You'll be fuel
For the wrong traveler
- /ˈmärSHən/

My rays will radiate
Even if my galaxies stop telling stories
I won't stay in this state
No matter how much the cosmos implores me
- /ˈmärSHən/

ORANGE

HAPPINESS

This pen is for all my smiles
The ones that can't be denied
It's for the days that I wake up
And God has already shared a joke with me
The days my heart can be felt when you walk by me
This pen is for my happiness
The one thing that won't be taken from me again
 -/ˈmärSHən/

She was my reset button
The prayer from last night
And the sun that greeted me this morning
I hope I'm the only flower she sees in sight
-/ˈmärSHən/

You're his Moroccan drums
Vibing through his whole body
Nothing else really matters because he's your man
And you are his girl
A queen to a man
A world to a boy
On a simpler level
His everything
-/ˈmärSHən/

If you were the sun
I would be the flowers stretching my pedals
To soak in your warm rays
You're my tree
My vines crawl and stick to you
In all different kinds of ways
-/ˈmärSHən/

Happiness is something I've failed to acknowledge
Because I've had a hard time letting go
Of the negative and embracing the positive
But I no longer want the bad to outshine the good
-/ˈmärSHən/

BALANCE
Just because I'm a happier person
Doesn't mean that my favorite days
Aren't still rainy ones
I need them
To wash off yesterday's anguish
So that my mind is clean
For the sunshine that is to come
-/ˈmärSHən/

As it pertains to love
I want to be struck by lightning
Filled with an electric current
That leaves my body glowing
With the charge of her affection
To power my heart
And illuminate my eyes
Encompassing her yellow aura
She would begin to brighten my days
-/ˈmärSHən/

Ripples of bliss
Is what it felt like
When we had our first kiss
-/ˈmärSHən/

I think I get lost in you
In smiles & all the happiness you offer for free
Your eyes are my favorite view
-/ˈmärSHən/

MAKE YOURSELF HAPPY FIRST
I think I spent too much time
Looking for something to make me happy
Whether that be a person
Friends
Or a new trend
I put my happiness in the wrong pot
-/ˈmärSHən/

I live in a cloud filled world
& it's only the days that I'm with you
That I catch a glimpse of the sun
-/ˈmärSHən/

LIGHT BLUE

<u>Calm</u>
I float when I write with you
I don't worry because it won't add another day to my life
Your tranquil waters put my chaotic mind at ease
This pen is the calming voice in my life
-/ˈmärSHən/

The first time you spoke I thought it was a song.
-/ˈmärSHən/

Oh, how this pen has saved me
The pages have made me feel sane
-/ˈmärSHən/

I free my emotions
Like the oceans
Waves are the voices of tides
Whether its low or high
I'm taking those white capes for a ride
Wild waves rise and fall
That's what makes this calm sea come alive
Now those blue giants thrill the rider who has surfed them
The water made me
Now waves cannot break me
I am the ocean
Everything else is just wind
-/ˈmärSHən/

Let your plans be as dark as night
Then strike
Like a lightning bolt
-/ˈmärSHən/

Your diamond studded structure has proved
Successful throughout battles you endured
The jade wall stands tall
No matter how bad it's been bruised over the years
It's matured
Guarding the embers to its fire has been a task untold
But soon a traveler will come and complement its stronghold
The sky will go dark and brighten time after time
But the doors won't open
Until the ruler sees the sapphire horizon
-/ˈmärSHən/

I'm free like a feather in the wind
It's been so long since I've been weightless
-/ˈmärSHən/

Sit back in silence
Then gain insight
-/ˈmärSHən/

I haven't been getting a lot of sleep lately
But I've still been able to go about my day
laughing, smiling, & all that good stuff
-
Even when you don't get the things you need
Or even an insufficient amount of it
You can still make it through the day
You can't attach too much weight to things
-/ˈmärSHən/

Get away from negativity
One of my best lessons to date
Is realizing my biggest problem was me
-/ˈmärSHən/

I write this from a different place
One higher than before
Not to say that my previous form brings me disgrace
But I can appreciate what seems to be the ceiling
After once more lying on the floor
-/ˈmärSHən/

DARK BLUE

NARRATIVE
For my deep blue days
When I think about my life
And how it's gotten to the place I'm standing today
I talk to myself in metaphors
And my heart's tears form the words on the pages.
The narrative of my life
-/ˈmärSHən/

It's crazy how much can change in a year, let alone a minute
Everything I thought I could plan for and it didn't even happen that way
Things catch you by surprise.
That's the scary thing
You can mean to be some place with all your might
But fate will take its path no matter what.
-/ˈmärSHən/

Pages
My release
My jail
My peace
My hell
Bound to feel these emotions
-/ˈmärSHən/

When I read poems someone always pops in my head
For every line there's a face
I can't help but get chills for the accuracy
It feels like I'm reading a story about them

The worst part is when I see myself
In a good poem but I'm the antagonist
I see the people I've hurt through these poems
These lines are my reflection.
-/ˈmärSHən/

The person that knows you
Immune to your manipulative ways
Does Not submit to the look in your eyes
And protects themselves from your cogent words
Is untouchable.
-/ˈmärSHən/

Sometimes I'm always looking
For something profound
I forget the little things
Mean just as much
-/ˈmärSHən/

Everyone turns somethings into nothings
But it's the nothings that seem to mean the most
Everything you're trying to let go of
Sticks to you and has nowhere else to go
-/ˈmärSHən/

Home is a locale in the mind
The spider web that houses a subconscious relaxation
A landscape
Traversed in radiance
Through thought
-/ˈmärSHən/

My eyes are my pen
And my mind is my paper
Some things I can't take off the lines
Realities are etched within my ink
When I write something down
It becomes real
So, I guess there are things I don't share
With anybody
Even myself
They just get locked away in my mind along with myself
Almost as if I'll get in trouble
For being me
-/ˈmärSHən/

You know when you lose a balloon
And you just kinda watch it leave the atmosphere?
Like "damn I kinda wanted that a little longer"
But in all reality
You were never really attached to it at all
You just liked the thought of having the balloon
-/ˈmärSHən/

The complexity of a stranger
Not knowing anything about them
Or where they come from
To think that they could be anything in the world
-/ˈmärSHən/

Some days these pages can't save me
They drown me
Suffocate me
And hold me
Their blank stare is worse than the writers
They don't talk to me
My words mean nothing to the universe
-/ˈmärSHən/

I like to think of soulmates
Like a big drawer full of socks
Because everyone is looking for a match
And it's so hard to find one
So, you force yourself into a pair
And it's uncomfortable
Or one that feels way better than the other
So, you spend the rest of your time trying to find that sock
Sometimes even trying to fit into socks you've outgrown
-/ˈmärSHən/

OVERTIME
In the event
That love
Starts to feel like a job
What shall I do?
-/ˈmärSHən/

I'm trying to balance extremes
Because I feel like I don't have in betweens
-/ˈmärSHən/

BLEU
Let the record play
To my blues symphony
So my mind can unravel what it has to say
& by the end of the song you will gain sympathy

For my guitar
The people who have strummed it
& plucked the strings
Until it bled into art
It's these moments I revisit

When I'm searching for strength
Because weakness has abducted me
Causing me to keep everyone at arm's length
These brown eyes are the bearers of pain you see

For all to hear
I hum my blues symphony
As the new day begins to disappear
The shadows set me free
-/ˈmärSHən/

I've always said expectations will get you hurt
But without expectation there is no standard
So, is it better to be a mountain in the wind?
Or pebbles in the river?
-/ˈmärSHən/

I GOT A QUESTION
In the world of poetry
Why isn't the poet ever completely healed?
They turn to the writing
But they are stuck here forever
Forever writing their angers out
With short breaks of happiness
They turn into their writing eternally
-/ˈmärSHən/

RED

<u>Love</u>
This pen is my softest voice
Elegant like a spider's web
Yet a ferocious beast
Trying to tame the solar flares
Of my heart that represent love
-/ˈmärSHən/

Hey flower,
Your magenta flames lick my skin
& bring color to my days
My sweet soft petal hand in hand
Even on a cloudy day the sun is still there
But you need rain to grow.

Everything that stems from you is alluring
It makes all the bad things worth enduring.
-/ˈmärSHən/

Two architects
As long as they both have the same vision
Anything they're building will be established
It doesn't matter if it crumbles once or twice
Because they've built the foundation first
Forever working there is no end
Making new creations as they come across them
Each one to be a reminder of where they've been.
-/ˈmärSHən/

You are
terrifyingly beautiful
A nuclear bomb
Exploding with the northern lights
-/ˈmärSHən/

I can't sing
But my words do
I'll write for you
From the depths of me

I can't paint
But my words do
I'll write for you
From the hues of my mind
My words will paint you with strokes

I can't dance
But my words do
I'll write for you
From the rhythm of my heart

I can't
But the poet can
-/ˈmärSHən/

Your smile sets ripples across calm waters,
I can see myself in the reflection of your heart
Scattering the colors of love
Endear you as a whole
Or don't endear you at all
Love you with my heart
Not just my eyes
When you smile
I fall
Where the mind doesn't think
The eyes never see clearly
And the butterflies never leave
Choose to love faithfully when all is awry
And loving us will feel right
-/ˈmärSHən/

LOVE
Crimson ocean,
Wash against me, perpetual waves
I am the shore
As you retreat
Bring a portion of me back with you every time

Low tide,
Let me walk deep into you
Let me learn about you
The things that live through you
And thrive off your body
Let my toes sink in the sand
without trepidation of what lies deeper

High tide
Drown me in your fervent current
Take me far
Keep me warm
Navigate me through your swells
And if my ship should wreck
Teach me to swim in your choppy waters
When you become too strenuous to swim in
Allow me to tread
While I catch my breath

When my lungs fill
Hold my back and let me float
Do not let me die
Ripple calmly into my cuts
Keep me silent
As I retire for the night
Become white noise in my subconscious and psyche
Robust. Benevolent. Consuming.
-/ˈmärSHən/

HIBERNATION

I know of a tree that thrives in a dead forest
You would look past it or give up
On trying to find it
If you were a seeker
Many have tried to unveil the secrets
Many have believed there was no tree there to begin with
Although the tree is waiting to rebirth things surrounding
To have been discovered
-/ˈmärSHən/

"WHAT'S YOUR FAVORITE THING ABOUT ME?"
Your eyes
Because that is the doorway
To your heart
The place where love resides
You are like raindrops on flowers
Wild, rare, beautiful, and surprising
Through layers of warmth
I see beyond your smile
-/ˈmärSHən/

I hope that our love
Would be like steps in the dark
With each one
You'd know you wouldn't fall
Eventually
We could run
-/ˈmärSHən/

I want to write notes through poems
Feel love through stanzas
-/ˈmärSHən/

"You're beautiful"
-An understatement
-/ˈmärSHən/

FERRIS WHEEL
At the top we get stuck in each other's eyes
& the cool breeze blows the scent of your perfume by my nose
Where it's just us
& the light of our smiles
To illuminate the night
As our feet dangle
-/ˈmärSHən/

UNIVERSAL
They say beauty is in the eye of the beholder
But you're in everyone's eyes
The stars in everyone's skies
-/ˈmärSHən/

YOUR SMILE
It mesmerizes me
Like the sunset on the mission beach horizon
Everyone stops to look at you
& they wonder
How heaven got to earth
-/ˈmärSHən/

SECRET GARDEN
You've found my door
Enter
See the petals of passion filling the floor
Be my Gardner
Trim my roses of romance
Water my tulips of tuition
Pick my lilies of love
And frolic through my sunflowers of radiance
-/ˈmärSHən/

SELF-LOVE
This love is my skin
The passion & patience is the moisture locked within
& it's so smooth because I bathe in the rays of kindness
They say black don't crack
So, my melanin is timeless
-/ˈmärSHən/

You could summon my spirit at any moment
Because I'm yours
After all these years our aura kept growing
We are magnetic to each other
-/ˈmärSHən/

I'm trying to make sure
That the moon & stars are aligned
Perfect in your universe
Because you are my world
-/ˈmärSHən/

MAROON

MARTIAN
This pen is for my abstract thoughts
The days I walk alone and observe
From a planet away
I find joy in my independence
Being a Martian
-/ˈmärSHən/

<u>4 Planets away</u>
On mars, there is no life
Only volcanic activity to brighten my night
Eruptions have a bad connotation
But these magma motifs are my inspiration
I'm Picasso on paper
Painting my mind through poetry
In the midst of this Crimson Vapor
-/ˈmärSHən/

SEATBELT SIGN IS ON
Racing against the sun
A sea of lights launches us
200 miles into the skies
And we float
Until the earthquake wakes us up
-/ˈmärSHən/

<u>EMERGENCY EXIT</u>
There's only one thing good about being a Martian....
When the visitors leave it's not so bad
You've lived there alone all your life
It's what you expect
When the next one comes you know not to get attached
The goodbyes become easy.
-/ˈmärSHən/

MARS
This is the place that I love best
A little green emerald in a king's chest
Hid among grasses and vines and trees
Summer retreat of the birds and bees

This is the place that I feel unassailable
Amidst words that epitomize wings
A spirit that makes fire sustainable

This is the place the storm doesn't rain
Between two cocoa cities
Eyes to grey matter galaxy
Wrapped in the colors of peace

This is the place I become that of pulp
Just enough that you should chew on me
And ponder my exclusivity

This is the place that I burn
Melted to my oils
To paint the pictures of eternity
In your mind
Forever glowing ember
This is my home
-/ˈmärSHən/

CREASES
I'm stuck between them
Trying to find my voice
-/ˈmärSHən/

The clouds followed by thunder and a flash of lightning
That's my sunny day
-/ˈmärSHən/

Revealing the layers to his soul
At the depths
Love

Not to be confused with the journey there
The black hole
The warm sea is paradoxical to the icicles above

No understanding can be gained
From the pictures painted on the walls
He plays a song with his broken heart strings
And that's what fills the windy halls
His abstract mind sings
-/ˈmärSHən/

Pastel hues
For my artistic views
Complacent in lavender
Even though I'm the mahogany traveler

I can't let go of this pain
It's taking up space in my brain
Rooted in me deep
Taking hours of my sleep

To switch now is madness
That would mean a blank canvas
A new artist in a new space
I'd have a new feeling to embrace

I think I like suffering in this place
-/ˈmärSHən/

EXTRATERRESTRIAL LOVE

When I look into your eyes, I see the stars
I dance on the rings of Jupiter & wait for your hand on the other side of Mars
If you read my book, you'd know my secrets & the atmosphere I live in
Originally from Earth but pain has thrust me to Venus
I am an itinerant being
My spirit is air within palms
But you seize me when I'm dreaming
I pray those plummeting celestial bodies bring you into my orbit
No matter the galaxies I enter or the constellations I leave
Don't ever change courses
If you should get stuck in my story
Let your heart be your bookmark
So that you'd always know your place
Stain my pages
Marking your territory
And your eyes would close in bliss
You would never wake up
Because you'd be dead by the thousandth kiss
-/ˈmärSHən/

My aura is moonlight
Which glows in the dark
Painting the night
With a lightning arc
-/ˈmärSHən/

MAHOGANY TRAVELER
Stay wild moon child
& don't be afraid to explore the universe
Because if you think Earth is the only habitable place
Then you have not discovered the galaxies of crimson
And the constellations within them
You have not been burned by the hypergiant
Nor cooled by the Ganymede moon
So, I encourage you to lay waste to everything you thought you knew
And float
Until the stars are all you know
-/ˈmärSHən/

MAHOGANY TRAVELER PT II
I went to Mars
& bought some real estate
Where the street lights are stars
& the chalk on the sidewalk doesn't fade
The sky is cotton candy
And the atmosphere is tranquility
-/ˈmärSHən/

It's so easy for me to detach
To leave the atmosphere
And hold my breath in space
While I orbit in the cold
-/ˈmärSHən/

Sometimes I feel like the universe
Because people see the colorful cracks of my spirit
& I'm too much to understand
& because your telescope doesn't see through flesh and bone
You make of it what you will
You see the stars and it attracts you
But soon you realize
The galaxy can't be bought
-/ˈmärSHən/

I'm jet pack joy riding
Through my crimson vapor
-/ˈmärSHən/

Could it be that I belong in space?
Because I feel like God is pulling me closer to him
On Earth I had a hard time finding my place
But in this atmosphere
I can feel the ice beginning to take over my face
-/ˈmärSHən/

I do life alone
It's better for the damage control
Since the last wreck I've grown
But trying to pick up the pieces every time
Isn't the end goal
-/ˈmärSHən/

Originally these writings were for me
But I'm sure someone will relate
-/ˈmärSHən/

www.ingramcontent.com/pod-product-compliance
Lightning Source LLC
Chambersburg PA
CBHW022115040426
42450CB00006B/714